GANDHI GOING GLOBAL 2019

Memories

A CELEBRATION OF GANDHIJI'S 150TH BIRTH ANNIVERSARY

ISBN: 978-81-246-1026-8

Images courtesy of Gandhi Research Foundation
Gandhi Teerth, Jain Hills, Jalgaon MH 525001, India. Tel: +91 257 226 0033. Web: gandhiresearch.org

Designed by Hitesh Shah, NuCreations.com

Printed in India by Shailee Creations LLP, +91-9871394810, creations.shailee@gmail.com

Preface

Fondly, popularly, and reverentially called "Father of the Nation", Mahatma Gandhi aka M.K. Gandhi aka Mohandas Karamchand Gandhi was a universal icon par excellence of truth, integrity, non-violence, love and compassion. His love for humanity knew no limits.

An anti-colonial nationalist, M.K. Gandhi was born on October 2, 1869, in Porbandar, Gujarat, into a well-known, influential Gujarati Hindu family. His father Karamchand Gandhi was the *dewan* (chief minister) of the then principality of Porbandar. After his schooling, giving up studying at the Samaldas College in Bhavnagar, he set out to become a barrister and joined the Inner Temple College, London, to study law. During his stay in England, along with his studies, he was deeply concerned with many personal and moral issues. It was in England that he read the Bible and the *Bhagavadgita* for the first time. These books were a solution to his many personal and moral problems. The *Bhagavatgita* influenced him so much that it became his life force guiding him all through his life. Its teaching on *karma-yoga* enlightened the hidden spirit in him and thus the *Bhagavatgita* became his personal guide and teacher.

Upon becoming a barrister, Gandhi returned to India in 1891. His aspiration to become a legal professional could not fructify. In addition, the legal profession was overcrowded. This made Gandhi to take up a legal job in Natal, South Africa, in 1893. This new domain gave him more challenges and opportunities alike. In Natal, he had to meet the worst face of apartheid being assaulted and thrown out of a train compartment meant only for the While despite him having a first-class ticket. It was here that Gandhi realized his inner strength and charted out strategies against racial discrimination and bonded labor. His reading of *Unto This Last* of John Ruskin and the "Sermon on the Mount" gave a new social perspective to him. Now he was determined to defend his dignity as an Indian and as an individual.

The pitiable condition of the South Asians as indented labor and the apartheid against the local Africans ignited his inner spirit of a *karma-yogin*. He organized the marginalized sections of the society and it was here he first put to use the non-violent civil disobedience as an expatriate lawyer in South Africa, in the resident Indian community's struggle for civil rights. It was an on-going up-down struggle for almost seven years. His relentless efforts with the support of South Asians, people of different walks and faiths, finally made the South

African government to change its policies. Gandhi left South Africa in 1914 and reached India in 1915. He was a persona par excellence by this time.

Now in India, the "realized" Gandhi set out to organize peasants, farmers, and urban laborers to protest against excessive land-tax and discrimination at the hands of the colonial rulers. The prevailing caste system pained him. However, he knew that a sudden change in the society's attitude was impossible. So he called those afflicted people *Harijan* (children of God). He was moved by the poverty and unhygienic living conditions prevailed all through the country. He found that India had lost her inner spirit, virtues and moral values at the hands of foreign rule.

Gandhi assumed the leadership of the Indian National Congress in 1921. At the outset, he had multiple challenges to address freedom for self-governance, well-being of India's common people, and their spiritual, educational and social emancipation. India had almost lost its age-old culture, educational system, its village economy structure, self-reliance, etc. He led nationwide campaigns for various social causes and for achieving *swaraj* (self-rule). Gandhi led Indians in challenging the British-imposed salt tax with the 400 km (250 miles) Dandi Salt March in 1930, and later in calling for the British to Quit India in 1942. He was imprisoned for many years, upon many occasions, in both South Africa and India.

He believed in village economy and its self-reliance. *Charkha* was its mascot. He led a modest life in a self-sufficient residential community and wore the traditional Indian *dhoti* and shawl, woven with yarn hand-spun on a *charkha*. He ate simple vegetarian food, and undertook long fasts as a means of both self-purification and political protest. Whenever there were social crises, he lived among the people and gave strength to people at times even making his close people uncomfortable. He hated greed and fought against it with tooth and nail.

He was a Hindu in letter and spirit. However, that did not stop him from loving and caring others. He absorbed everything good from other religions and societies and assimilated them to his core strength. He was very secular in approach and attitude. He donned different caps, of a politician, a social reformer, an economist, an educationalist, and a spiritual guide, above all a true human being. He believed in soul-force than in physical force.

His vision of a clean, hygienic, and healthy India was the prelude to our Prime Minister Narendra Modi's well-acknowledged Swatch Bharat program. We have achieved spectacular progress in this mission while we are celebrating the 150th Birth Anniversary of Mahatma Gandhi.

What makes Mahatma Gandhi stand tall among other leaders of modern times? First, he was not power hungry. Two, he lived among people as a common man. Three, truth and simplicity were his virtues. Four, non-violence was his weapon. Fifth, he was ready to review his decisions and make changes as and when required. Sixth, he was well aware of his moorings.

More importantly, he could address or even support issues intelligently and sensibly. For example, he supported the British administration in the Boer War of South Africa and in the two world wars, though he was totally against the colonial rule. Our modern-day politicians do not have this quintessential character in addressing many an issue of national/international importance.

That is why he found followers among towering personalities of the world such as Martin Luther King Jr., Nelson Mandela, Albert Einstein, Steve Jobs, Mother Theresa, and Barrack Obama.

Non-violence, communal harmony, self-discipline, and self-reliance are some of the core values the present world should adapt from the Mahatma, and his teachings and philosophies are the only remedy for the burning issues we face every day nationally and globally.

All these make him a *mahatma* (a great soul), indeed!

This pictorial volume, brought out on the 150th birth anniversary of Mahatma Gandhi, takes one through the inspiring life journey of a great, noble soul. Happy reading!

Acknowledgments

A project of this dimension demands a lot of planning and support of varied nature. Our effort at the Gandhian Society to bring out this pictorial volume on the 150th birth anniversary of Mahatma Gandhi could not have been possible sans the cooperation, encouragement and support – creative, financial, intellectual – of a few dedicated, philanthropic persons. Though we cannot ink and acknowledge all of them in person, it will be an error if we leave out to recognize a few of them. Our special mention and acknowledgment are due to

ADITYA BIRLA GROUP
ALBERT JASANI & SOBHANA PATEL
DANNY GAEKWAD
Dr. NAVIN MEHTA
DIPAK & NAYANA SHAH
KENNY DESAI
MUKUND THAKAR
RASHMI & MAHESH PATEL
KALPANA V PATEL
RCD CHECK CASHING & FINANCIAL SERVICES
A & R INFOTECH
BRIDGEWATER SENIORS COUNCIL
CHAMBORD INC
Drs. ARCHANA & DEEPAK NARAN
GOLDEN ERA
HASMUKH PATEL
INDIAN CULTURAL SOCIETY OF NJ
KRIYAA WHOLESALE
RANJAN & JAYANTKUMAR PATEL
SVAJAN
UNITED MORTGAGE MART
UNITY BANK

Further, we place on records our sincere gratitude to the Gandhi Research Foundation, India, for its incredible support, making us available the images used in this volume. The pictures give the collector's issue a biographical look on the life and times of Mahatma Gandhi. In addition, we acknowledge the efforts and support of Mr. Hitesh Shah for its design.

Gandhian Society

Gandhian Society believes in following values (Gandhian Way of Living):

- *Ahimsa* – Nonviolence
- *Satya* – Truth
- *Asteya* – Non-stealing
- *Brahmacarya* – Self-discipline
- *Aparigraha* – Non-possession
- *Sharirshrama* – Self labor
- *Aswada* – Control of the palate
- *Sarvatra Bhayavarjana* – Fearlessness
- *Sarva Dharma Samanatva* – Equality of all religions
- *Swadeshi* – Use locally made goods
- *Sparshbhavana* – Remove untouchability

Vision

The vision of Gandhian Society is to make teachings of Mahatma Gandhi available and accessible to everyone, especially to our youth. To raise awareness towards the non-violence approach and "Bring the Change by Being the Change". Opening a "free" museum and activity center displaying the life and works of Gandhiji. Providing a platform to bring global scholars and researchers together in giving our community true teachings of Mahatma Gandhi.

Mission

Our core mission is

- Spread the message of non-violence, eradicate discrimination and implement Gandhian methodology and philosophy to uplift humanity.
- Support all the Gandhian associations and organizations doing similar work around the world and spread awareness all across the US.

The opportunity to spread this message around Gandhiji's birth anniversary . . .

Thus was born Gandhi Going Global!

What We Do?

The Gandhian Society (GS) exists to promote the Gandhian Way of Life in USA. We spread his message of non-violence, truth, self-discipline and love, among the people of America.

To inform, educate and engage the residents and future generations GS has designed a yearlong campaign on his 150th birth anniversary called Gandhi Going Global or G3. It includes, an expo, a museum, a souvenir shop as well as Motivational Talks, Interactive and Introspective Activities, Educational Programs, Cultural Celebrations, and more.

We hope that through these activities the participants will absorb the 11 Rules of Life, followed by Gandhiji himself and be inspired to make a difference by "being the change".

bapu

c. 1936

A UNIQUE COLLECTION OF RARE IMAGES OF MAHATMA GANDHI.

Images in this publication are maintained close to their original quality.

Mahatma Gandhi reading, as he sits next to a traditional spinning wheel, Harijan Colony, Delhi, April 1946.

All the great religions of the world inculcate the equality and brotherhood of mankind and the virtue of toleration.

- Mahatma Gandhi

Mahatma Gandhi (top center) with co-founders of the Natal Indian Congress, Durban, 1895.

Mahatma Gandhi sitting with his private secretary, Ms. Sonia Schlesin (right) and Henry S. Polak (left) in front of his office at Rissik & Anderson Streets, Johannesburg, 1905.
Standing behind Gandhi: Coopoo Moonlight Moodley (left).

As a barrister wearing the London Vegetarian Society's badge, Johannesburg, 1906.

Mahatma Gandhi, Sonia Schlesin and Dr. Hermann Kallenbach, before the 'Historic March' from Natal to Transvaal, 1913.

This photograph was carried by Kallenbach to England folded and stitched into the collar of his suit, as he was afraid to get it confiscated, due to his German origin.

Pioneer settlers of Tolstoy Farm, 1910.

Standing from right:
L. Ramsamy, Ponsamy, L.M. Morgan, Venugopal Naidoo, C.K.T. Coopoo Naidoo and K. Devar.

Sitting from right:
Pragjee Desai, Rajee Naidoo, Joseph Roypen, Dr. Hermann Kallenbach, Mahatma Gandhi, Mrs. P.K. Naidoo, Mrs. Lazarus, Mrs. C.K. Thambie Naidoo.

Third row:
Bala, Bhartasarathy, Naransamy and Puckry Naidoo (all sons of Thambie Naidoo).

Members of the reception committee during the visit of Gopal Krishna Gokhale to South Africa, Durban, October 1912. Below row, center, from left: Dr. Hermann Kallenbach, Mahatma Gandhi, Gokhale, Parsee Rustomjee.

Pretoria Passive Resisters with striped jerseys, vs. Johannesburg Passive Resisters with plain jerseys played in Rangers Ground, Mayfair, Johannesburg, 1913.

First Row:
Standing from left: Unknown, S.B. Medh, Murugas (Thabla) Naidoo, Dr. Hermann Kallenbach, C.K. Thambi Naidoo (Chairman Transvaal Tamil Benefit Society), Mahatma Gandhi, Miss Sonja Schlesin, L.W. Ritch, G. Isacks, Khusal Bai, Sorabji, Shapurji.

Second Row:
Subraya Padayachy (Acting Chairman Pretoria Tamil League), Venogopal Naidoo, D. Lazarus, K. Raja Rethnam, Perumaal Naidoo, V.S. Manickum Pillay, Billy K.G. Pillay, Sooboo Naidoo, V. Chetty, Newyoki, V.S. Pillay (Chairman Pretoria Tamil League), Chinapa, R. Kathira Velloo Padayachy, J.K. Philips, H. Moonsamy.

Third Row:
Francis Pillay, Murugas Pillay, Govindsamy Masthan Padayachy, Johnny Peters, Ramlall Mooloo (Chairman Pretoria Indian Congress), N.K. Pillay (Johannesburg Captain), Boblal Maharaj (Pretoria Captain), G.H. Moona, David Anthony, V. Naidoo, David Mooideen, Narsoo Naidoo, David Ernest, N.S. Pillay.

Fourth Row:
R.R. Frank, John Andrews, H. Masootoo Pillay, K. Jaganathan Pillay, Chinsamy Pillay, Jimmy Chetty, D. Patel, S. Arunachala Padayachy, Aron John, Govindasamy Pillay.

Mahatma Gandhi at the volunteers' rallye, Belgaum Congress, December 1924.

Mahatma Gandhi at a meeting in Madras with Annie Besant and Srinavasa Sastri, September 1921.

Mahatma Gandhi in characteristic pose, 1924.

Mahatma Gandhi came to Madurai in 1924 where he stayed at the house of Barrister George Joseph. It was during that visit that he addressed a group which included many peasants. He noticed that most of them did not wear a shirt and barely enough of a lower garment to be called a dhoti. Gandhi asked Barrister George Joseph why people are dressed in that manner. He was told it was because they were impoverished and could not afford anything better.

This bothered Gandhi greatly and he apparently had a sleepless night. When he came down the next morning, he had shed his shirt and was wearing a dhoti. He said that it was his way of associating with the impoverished masses.

Mahatma Gandhi visiting the physical institute in Dhulia, February 13, 1927.

Mahatma Gandhi and Jawaharlal Nehru, 1929.

Mahatma Gandhi walking with a foreigner, c. 1929.

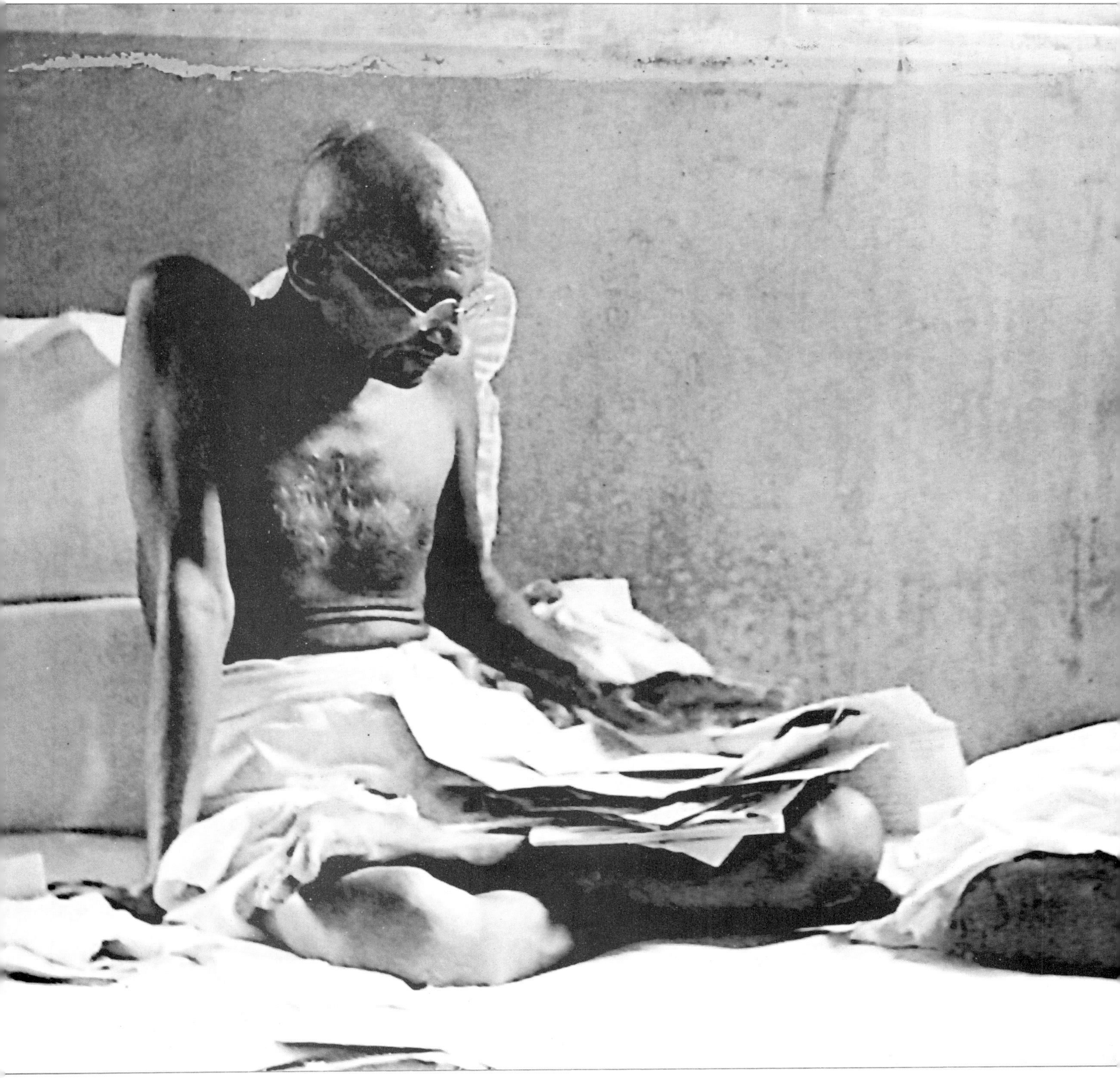

Mahatma Gandhi attending to his correspondence at Mani Bhavan, Bombay, 1929.

Sarojini Naidu receiving Mahatma Gandhi during Salt Satyagraha at Dandi, April 5, 1930.

First they ignore you, then they ridicule you, then they fight you, and then you win.

- Mahatma Gandhi

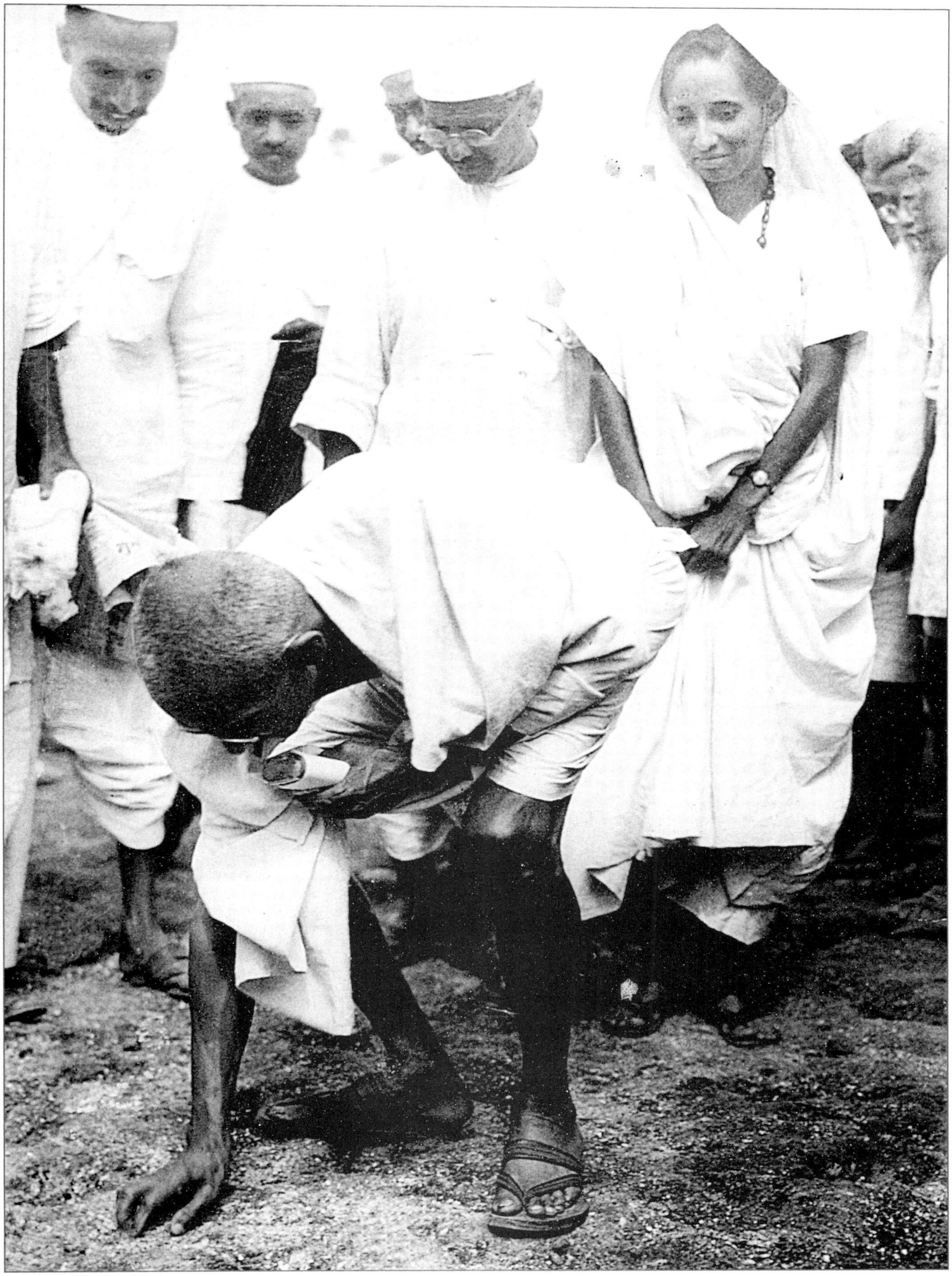

Mahatma Gandhi breaking the salt law by picking up a lump of natural salt at Dandi, April 6, 1930, 8.30 a.m.

Mahatma Gandhi playing with a child during his voyage to England on board of SS Rajputana, August 1931.

Mahatma Gandhi in conference with Rajendra Prasad and Acharya J.B. Kripalani at Swaraj Bhavan, Allahabad, February 1931.

Mahatma Gandhi shortly before his departure to England at the mole, Bombay, August 29, 1931.

Women at right, from left: Manibehn Patel, Sarojini Naidu and Kasturba Gandhi.
2nd left: Madan Mohan Malaviya.

Mahatma Gandhi on the captain's bridge during his voyage to England on board of S.S. Rajputana, August 1931. Centre: Manibehn Patel; left: Capt. Morton Jack.

Mahatma Gandhi persuaded prisoners to give up hunger-strike in Delhi Jail, Delhi, March 15, 1939. Right: Mahadev Desai.

James Phillips, the Pearly King of Hoston (costermonger), and his son and daughter present a crane of South African oranges to Mahatma Gandhi when he leaves Kingsley Hall enroute to atttend the 2nd Round Table Conference, London, September 15, 1931.

Mahatma Gandhi bidding farewell to his countrymen from the promenade deck of S.S. Rajputana shortly before his departure to England, Bombay, August 29, 1931.

Also be seen (from left): Mirabehn, Sarojini Naidu and Madan Mohan Malaviya.

Do not judge others. Be your own judge and you will be truly happy. If you will try to judge others, you are likely to burn your fingers.

- Mahatma Gandhi

Mahatma Gandhi and Charles Chaplin conversing in the surgery of Dr. Katial in Backton Road, Canning Town, London, September 22, 1931.

This conversation formed the starting point to Chaplin's movie Modern Times.

Mahatma Gandhi and cheering mill workers while leaving one of the textile mills at Spring Vale, Darwen, Lancashire, UK, September 26, 1931. Also be seen: Mirabehn (4th right).

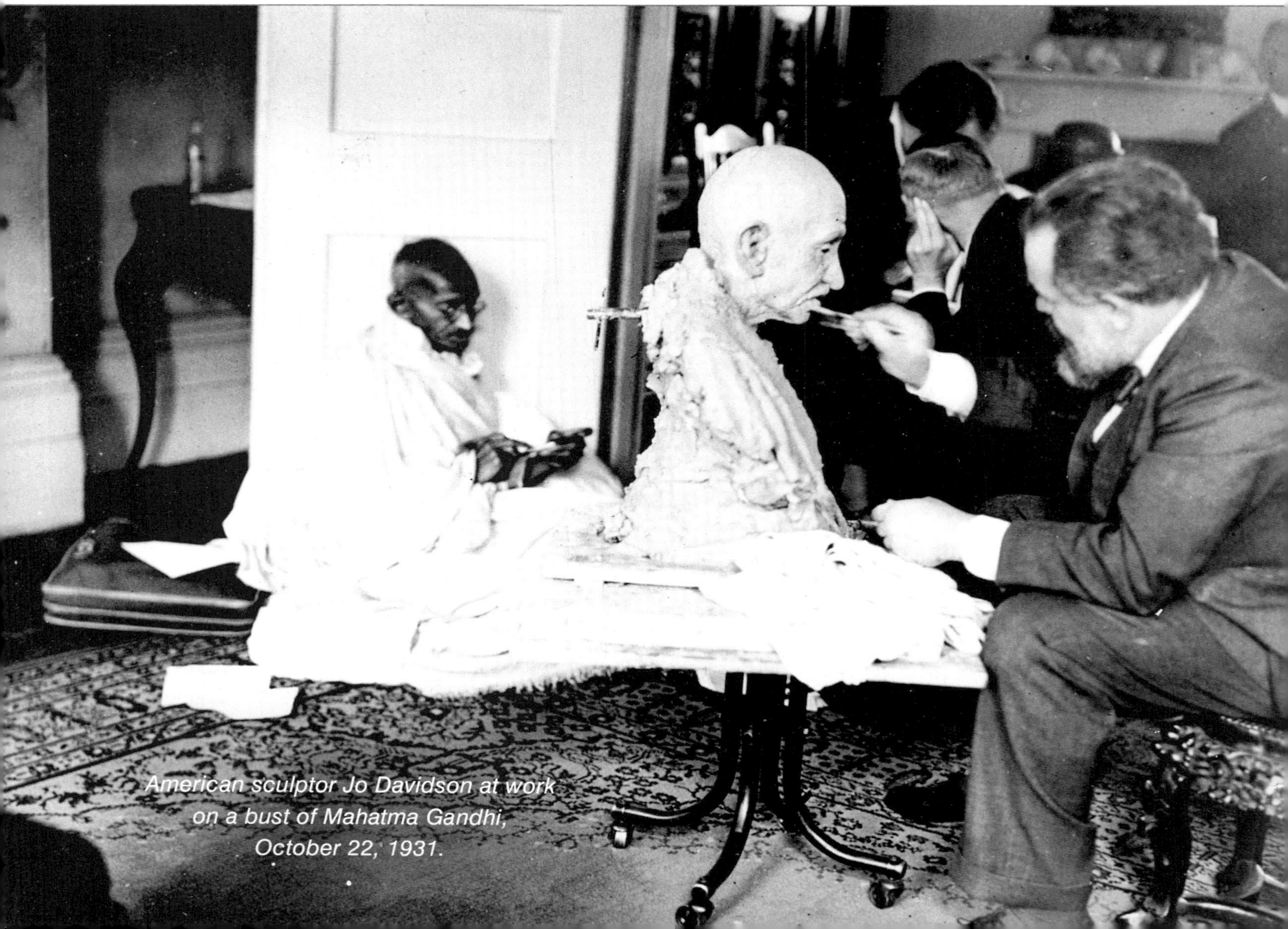

American sculptor Jo Davidson at work on a bust of Mahatma Gandhi, October 22, 1931.

Mahatma Gandhi alighting from S.S. Rajputana at Marseilles, September 11, 1931.

Mahatma Gandhi arrives in Canning Town, London, to meet Charles Chaplin. Gandhi is surrounded by East End admirers, September 22, 1931.

Mahatma Gandhi and Dr. Josiah Oldfield at the Frutarian Society's dinner, London, on October 23, 1931.

Strength does not come from physical capacity. It comes from an indomitable will.

- Mahatma Gandhi

Mahatma Gandhi recording his speech On God for Columbia Grammophone Company at Kingsley Hall, October 20, 1931.

From right:
2nd: Mahadev Desai; 3rd: Muriel Lester

Mahatma Gandhi talking with Romain Rolland in his villa Olga at Villeneuve-Montreux, Switzerland, December 6 or 9, 1931.

Front: Mirabehn.

Mahatma Gandhi addressing the public at Azad Maidan, Bombay, shortly after his return to India from UK, December 28, 1931.

The best way to find yourself is to lose yourself in the service of others.

- Mahatma Gandhi

Mahatma Gandhi during an interview of social workers at Satyagraha Ashram, Sevagram/Wardha, May 1936.

An unknown woman, Kahandas Gandhi, Mahatma Gandhi and Kasturba Gandhi walking at Satyagraha Ashram, Sevagram, 1939.

Mahatma Gandhi, during his convalescence, walking with others on Juhu Beach, Bombay, December 1937. Left: Dr. Sushila Nayar; right: Gandhi's grandson Kahandas (Kanaa, Kanu).

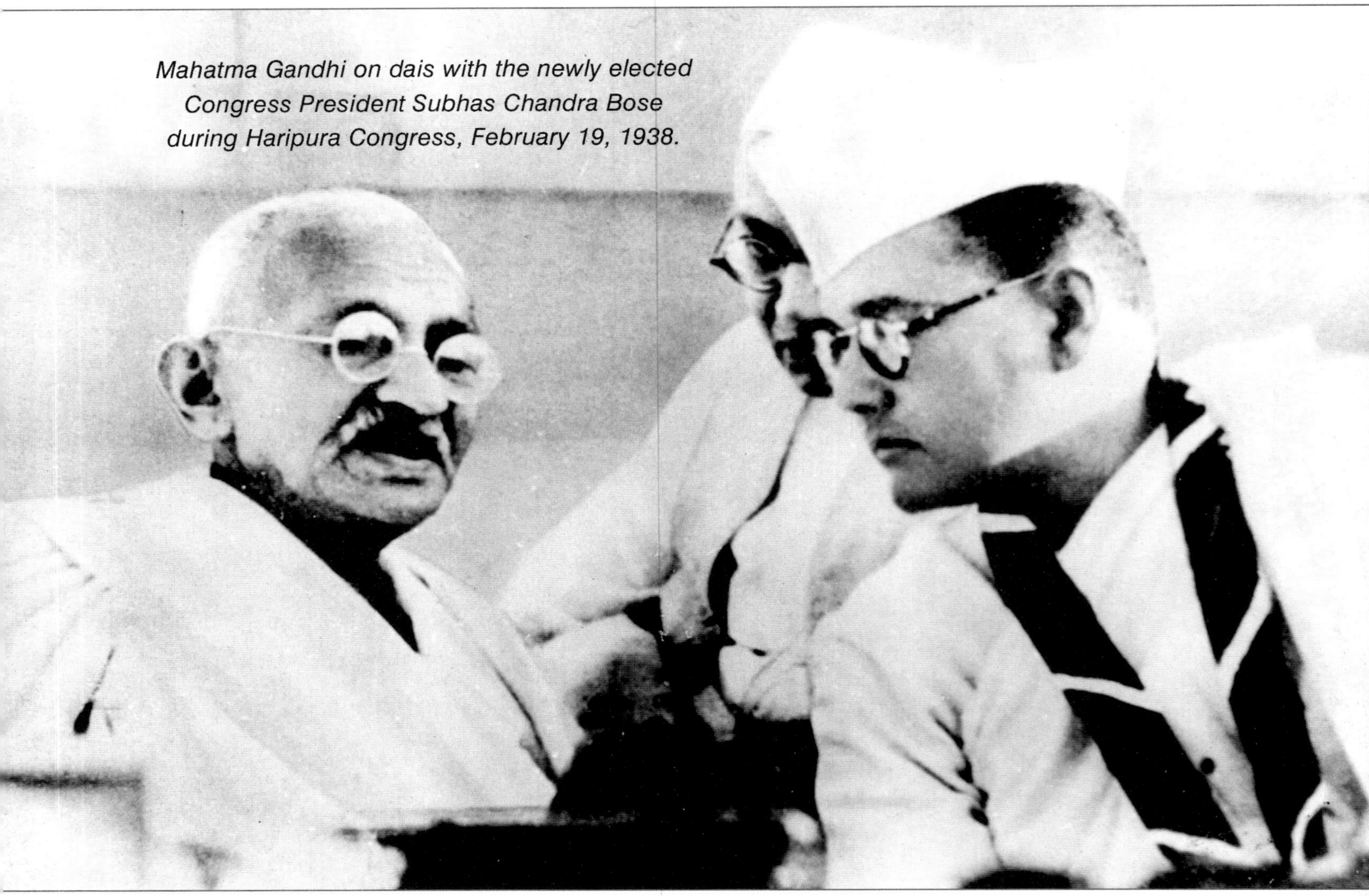

Mahatma Gandhi on dais with the newly elected Congress President Subhas Chandra Bose during Haripura Congress, February 19, 1938.

Mahatma Gandhi at Rajkot, February 1939.

Mahatma Gandhi greeting people from the train at Peshawar, November 1938.

Mahatma Gandhi with Mahadev Desai and others, c. 1938.

Mahatma Gandhi with Rabindranath Tagore at Santiniketan, West Bengal, February 18, 1940.

Mahatma Gandhi and Kasturba Gandhi with Rabindranath Tagore, Amra-Kunj, Santiniketan, West Bengal, February 18, 1940.

Mahatma Gandhi, Mahadev Desai, Dhirendra Chatterjee (brother of Abha Gandhi) and a visitor from USA at Satyagraha Ashram, Sevagram, 1940.

Mahatma Gandhi at the microscope observing leprosy germs at Satyagraha Ashram, Sevagram, c. 1940.

Students of Mahila Ashram (training centre for women founded by Jamnalal Bajaj) meet Mahatma Gandhi in front of his hut at Satyagraha Ashram, Sevagram after village cleaning campaign, 1941.

Mahatma Gandhi calling Amtus Salam in Bombay from the office hut at Satyagraha Ashram, Sevagram, 1940.

Mahatma Gandhi talking with US journalist Louis Fischer at Satyagraha Ashram, Sevagram, June 1942.

Mahatma Gandhi attending to leper patient Sanskrit scholar Parchure Shastri at Satyagraha Ashram, Sevagram, 1940.

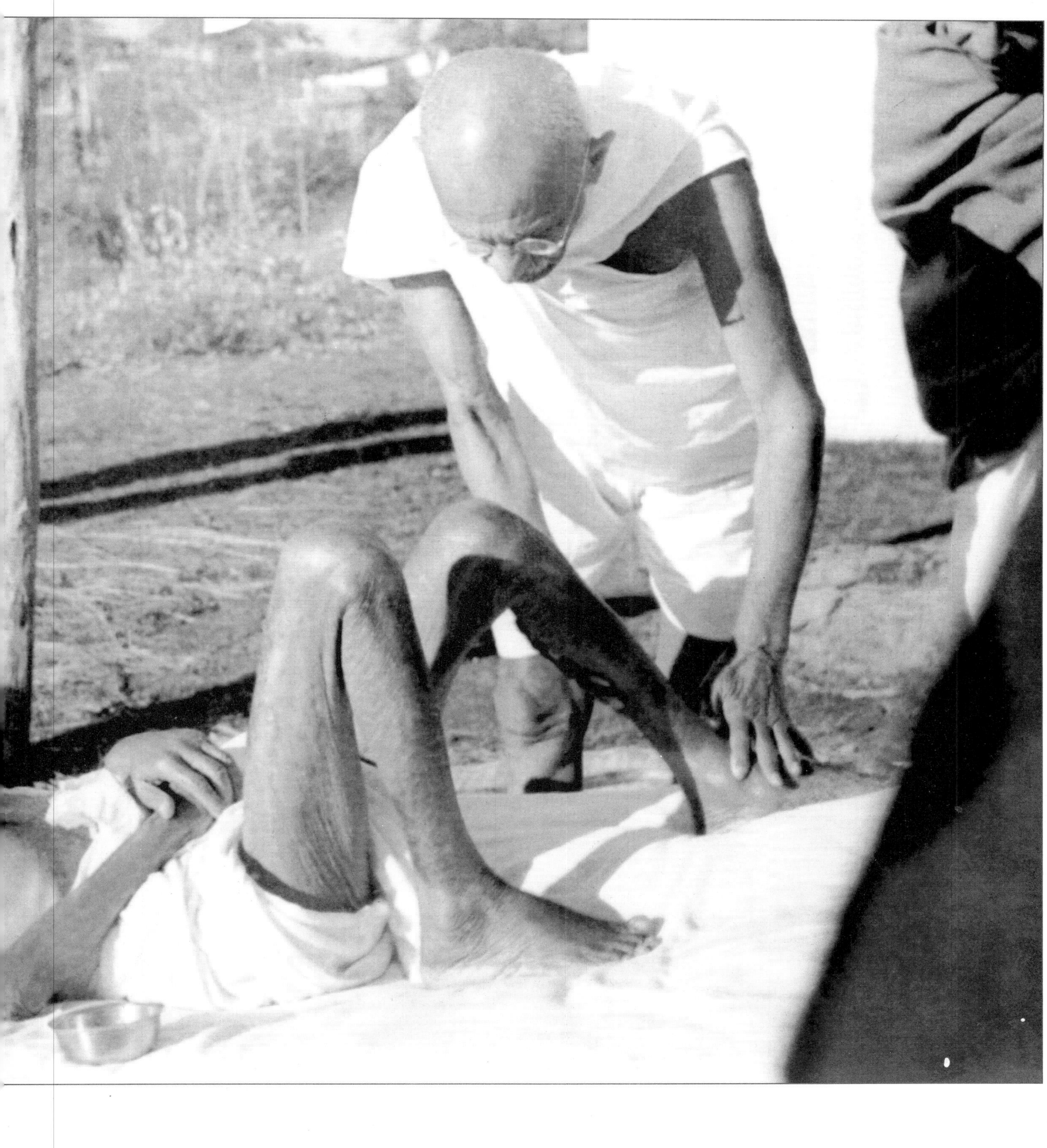

An eye for an eye will only make the whole world blind.

- Mahatma Gandhi

Mahatma Gandhi with associates in South Africa, 1914.

Mahatma Gandhi, c. 1940.

Women is the incarnation of Ahimsa. Ahimsa means infinite love.

- Mahatma Gandhi

Kasturba and Mahatma Gandhi (seated, centre) with a group of women 1913. Above and between Gandhi and Kasturba: Sonia Schlesin.

Mahatma Gandhi and Madan Mohan Malaviya at the Silver Jubilee Convocation at Benares Hindu University, Varanasi, January 21, 1942.

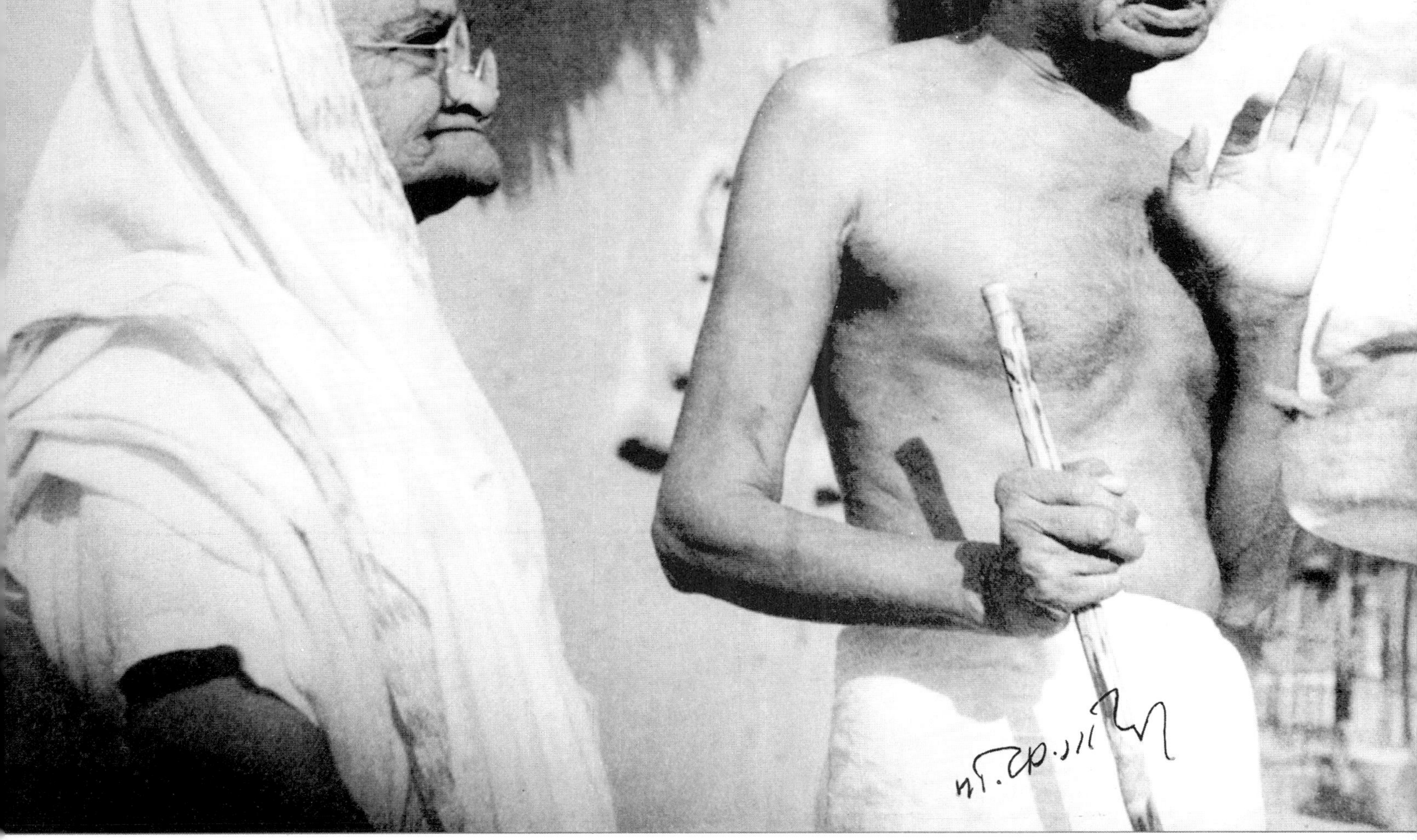

Mahatma Gandhi and Kasturba Gandhi at Satyagraha Ashram, Sevagram, January 1942.

Photograph carries Gandhi's signature in Gujarati.

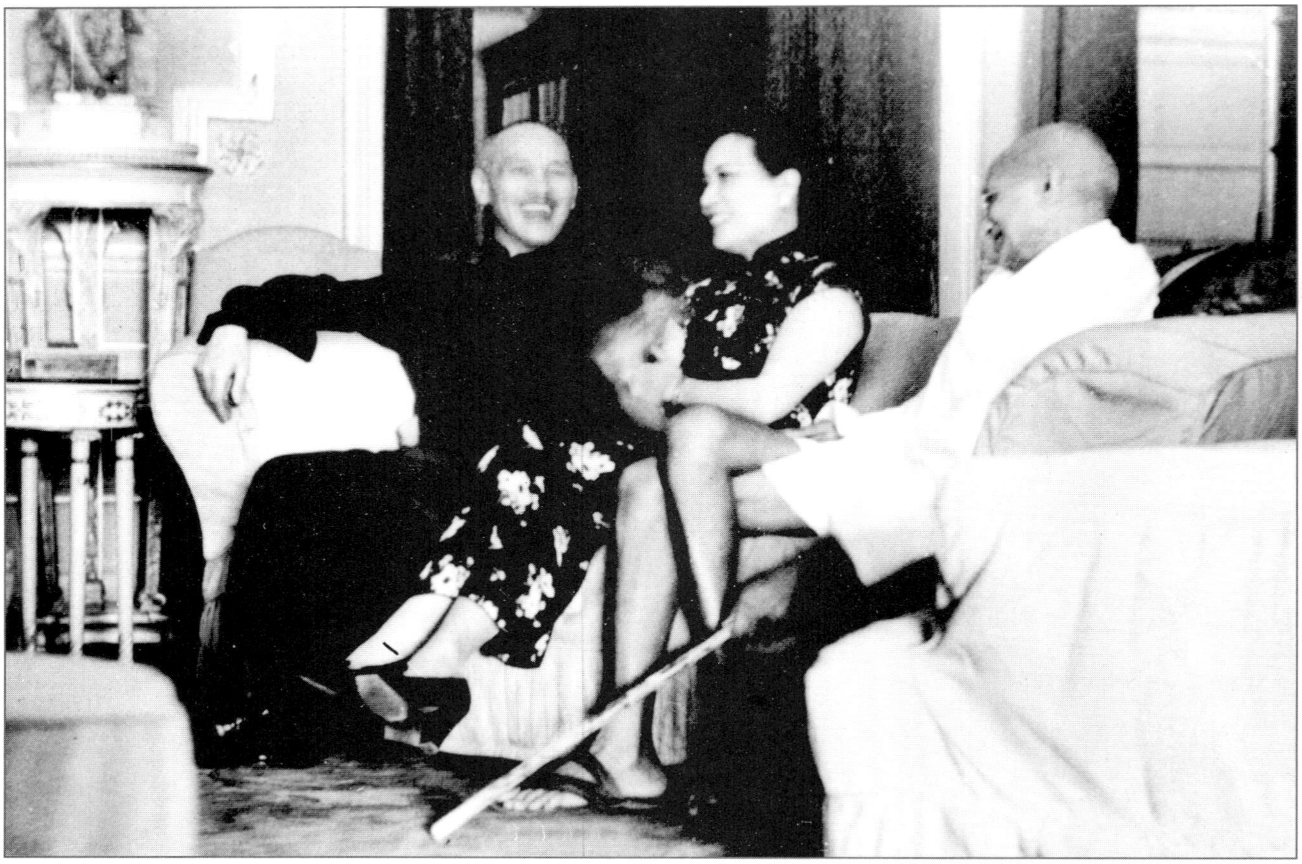

Mahatma Gandhi talking with Chinese leader Chiang Kai-shek and his wife in Calcutta, February 18, 1942.

Mahatma Gandhi and American journalist Louis Fischer at Satyagraha Ashram, Sevagram, June 1942.

Mahatma Gandhi is seen to his car by Sir Stafford Cripps after an over 2 hours lasting interview at 3, Queen Victoria Rad, New Delhi, March 27, 1942.

Mahatma Gandhi at the All-India Congress Committee meeting, August 8, 1942.

Also be seen: Abul Kalam Maulana Azad (centre right) and Pyarelal Nayar (back).

Passive resistance is a method of securing rights by personal suffering; it is the reverse of resistance by arms.

- Mahatma Gandhi

Mahatma Gandhi with Sardar Vallabhbhai Patel at the All-India Congress Committee meeting, August 8, 1942.

Also be seen: Mahadev Desai (right).

Mahatma Gandhi with Mahadev Desai (right) at the All-India Congress Committee meeting, August 8, 1942.

Mahatma Gandhi at a public meeting during Salt Satyagraha at Bhimrad, Surat district, April 9, 1930.

Truth is God.

- Mahatma Gandhi

Mahatma Gandhi distributing mangoes to children after prayer at Juhu Beach, Bombay, May/June 1944.

Mahatma Gandhi with his associates during a walk at Juhu Beach, Bombay, May/June 1944.

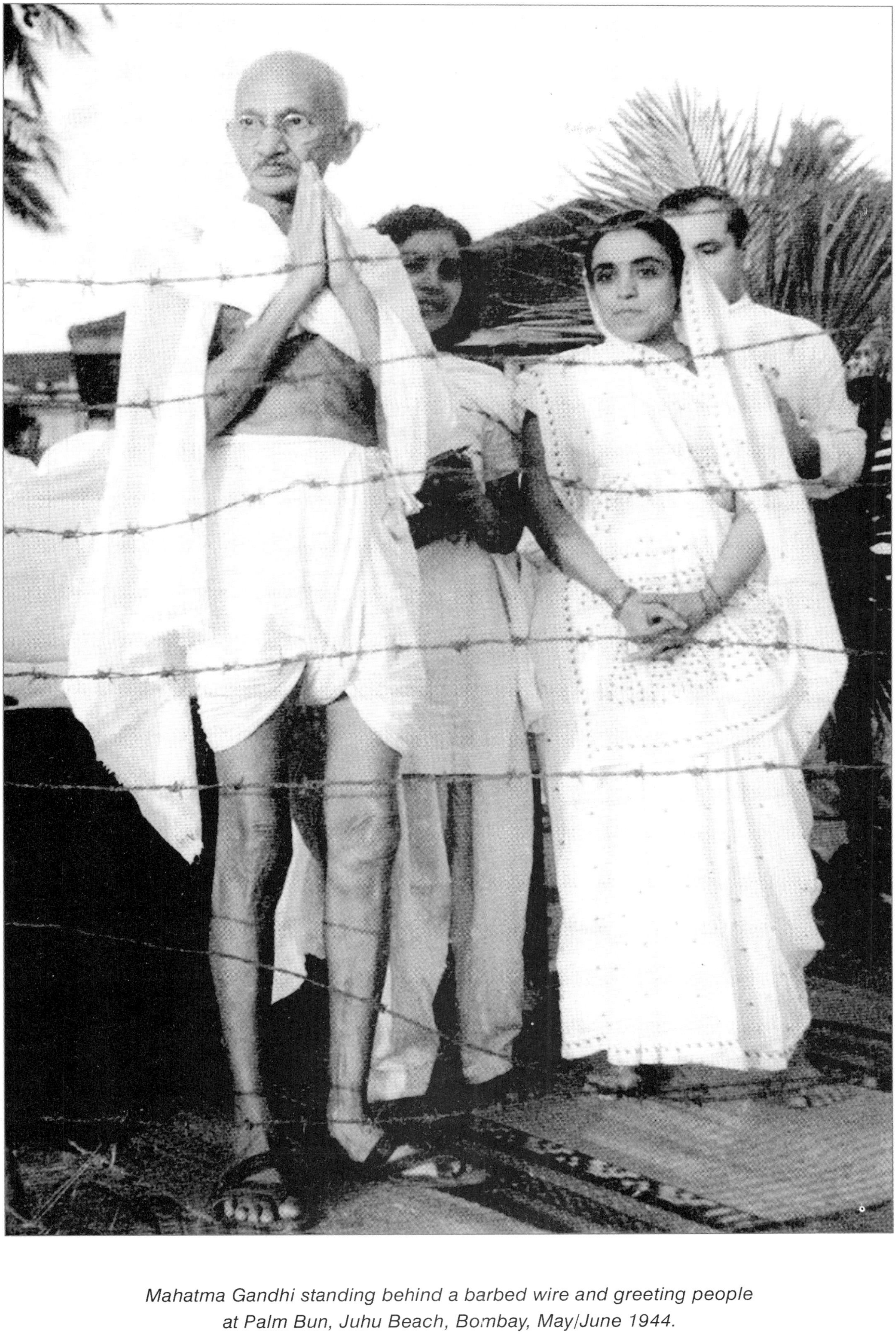

Mahatma Gandhi standing behind a barbed wire and greeting people at Palm Bun, Juhu Beach, Bombay, May/June 1944. Next to Gandhi from left: Dr. Sushila Nayar, his hostess, Sumati Morarjee and Dr. Dinshah Mehta.

Mahatma Gandhi collecting money for the Harijan Fund on his way to Poona, June 15, 1944.

Mahatma Gandhi sitting alone at Juhu Beach, Bombay, May/June 1944.

Mahatma Gandhi at a public prayer meeting in front of Rungta House, Bombay, September 1944.

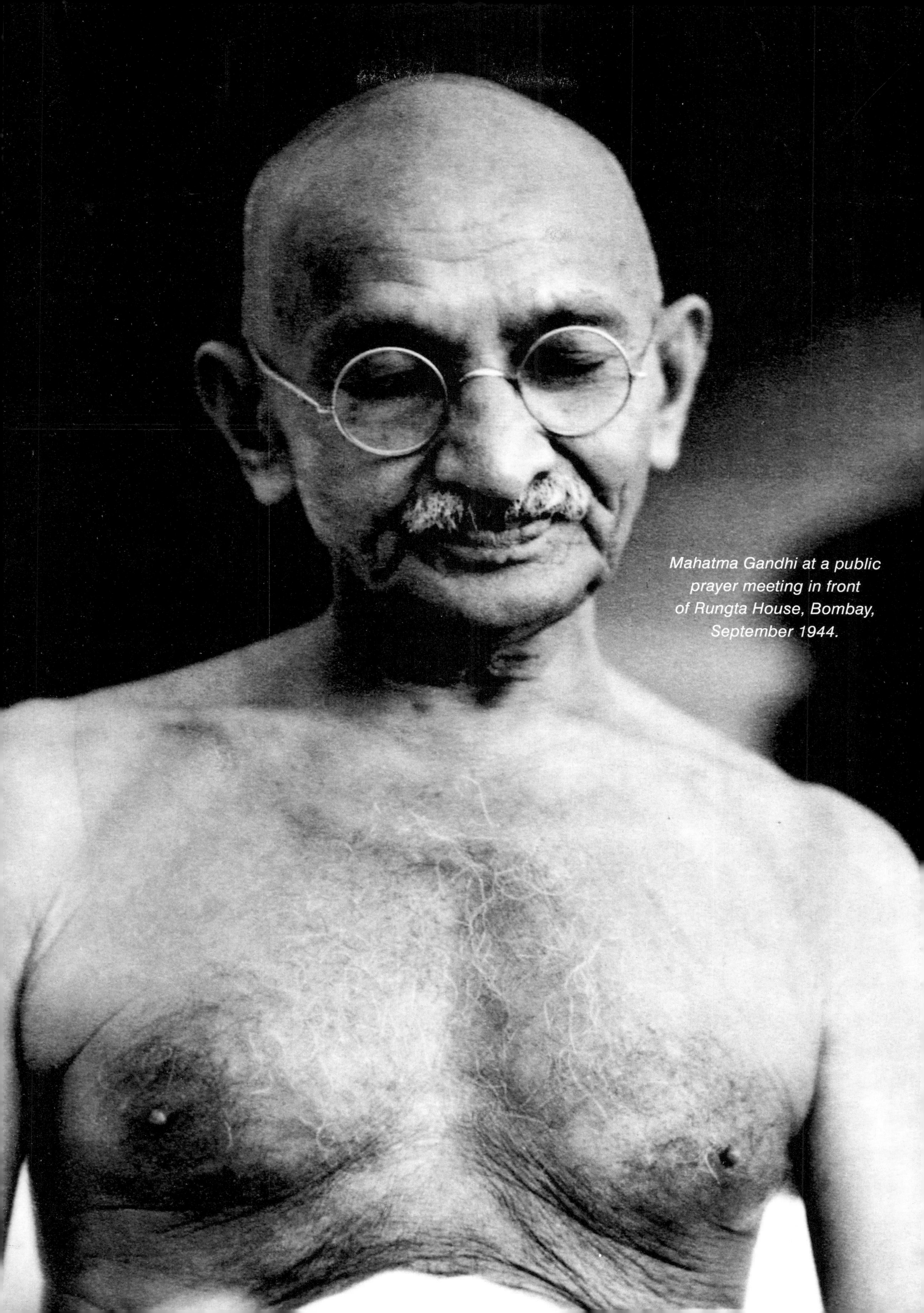

Mahatma Gandhi at a public prayer meeting in front of Rungta House, Bombay, September 1944.

Awaited by Sardar Vallabhbhai Patel (centre left), Mahatma Gandhi alighting from a train, 1944.

Mahatma Gandhi on way to meet the British Viceroy at Simla, June 24, 1945.

Mahatma Gandhi with HE R.G. Casey, Governor of Bengal, Calcutta, December 1, 1945.

Sudhir Ghosh (left), Ramkrishna Bajaj (centre) and Mahatma Gandhi on a boat on way to Midnapur (East Bengal), December 24, 1945.

Mahatma Gandhi addressing a public meeting at Mahishadal (East Bengal), December 25, 1945.

Mahatma Gandhi walking at Satyagraha Ashram, Sevagram, 1945.

Mahatma Gandhi surrounded by crowd during his visit of political prisoners at Dum Dum Jail, Calcutta, January 17, 1946.

A British parliamentary delegation meets Mahatma Gandhi at Madras, January 23, 1946.

Mahatma Gandhi during his Harijan tour in South India, January 1946.

Mahatma Gandhi giving darshan to the people from the train coach on his day of silence, February 1946.

Right: Chakravarti Rajagopalachari.

Mahatma Gandhi collecting donations for Harijan Fund with a basket in his hand at a train station on his way to Assam, January 1946.

Mahatma Gandhi and Lieutenant Colonel De M.S. Fraser (left), political aide to the Secretary of State for India, are shown after a 1 hour 25 minutes British cabinet meeting following discussions in reference to Indian independence.

At right is Alec H. Joyce, publicity director of the Secretary of State of India.

They are shown at the entrance to the Viceroy's lodge, New Delhi. April 3, 1946.

Herbert Hoover, nearing the end of his world-wide investigation of food conditions, leaves British Viceroy Lord Wavell's house with Mahatma Gandhi, following a conference on India's food problem. The former US-President said there is no present famine in India, but there will be if supplies are halted, April 24, 1946.

Mahatma Gandhi greets Sir Stafford Cripps at the Bhangi Colony, Delhi, April 1946.

Mahatma Gandhi sleeping in a train compartment, c. May 1946.

Mahatma Gandhi spinning at Khadi Pratisthan, Sodepur, Calcutta, October 1946.

Mahatma Gandhi spinning in the garden of Birla House, New Delhi, November 1947.

Mahatma Gandhi on his way to his peace mission in Noakhali, November 1946.

Mahatma Gandhi and his party during his visit to the riot-stricken areas in Noakhali, January 1947.

Gandhi leaning on Dr. Sushila Nayar (right) and Sushila Pai (left).

Also be seen: Jivan Singh (with turban; member of Indian National Army).

Mahatma Gandhi in the garden of Birla House, where he began a fast for communal peace in India, New Delhi, January 13, 1947. Left: Abha Gandhi.

Mahatma Gandhi during his peace march in Noakhali, November 1946.

Mahatma Gandhi on a morning walk with Khan Abdul Ghaffar Khan (left), Manu Gandhi and Captain Shah Nawaz Khan (right) on the compound of Dr. Saiyad Mohammed's bungalow at Patna, during Gandhi's peace march in Bihar, March 24, 1947.

A rare studio photograph of Mahatma Gandhi taken in London at the request of Lord Irwin, 1931.
Photograph carries Gandhi's signature in Gujarati.

Gandhi with us...

Gandhi within us...

Gandhian Society is a non-political, non-profit organization founded by Shri Bhadra Butala and like minded people who carry Gandhiji within their head, heart and in action.

We have three founding pillars... "Nonviolence, Communal Harmony and Self Discipline"

The objective of Gandhian Society is to spread Gandhian philosophy all across USA. Our belief is that Gandhiji's message is the solution for all the problems in the world.

The true vision of Gandhian Society is to make the thoughts of Gandhiji accessible to the youth, raise awareness towards the non-violence approach and 'Bring the Change by Being the Change'.

gandhian society

GANDHIAN SOCIETY
425 Lincoln Highway
Iselin, NJ 08830
732-407-5013
www.gandhiansociety.org

9 788124 610268